I AM NOT A CRYBABY

NORMA SIMON

Pictures by
HELEN COGANCHERRY

Albert Whitman & Company, Niles, Illinois

ALSO BY NORMA SIMON
All Kinds of Families
Cats Do, Dogs Don't
Children Do, Grownups Don't
How Do I Feel?
I Know What I Like
I'm Busy, Too
I Was So Mad
I Wish I Had My Father
Nobody's Perfect, Not Even My Mother
Oh, That Cat!
The Saddest Time
Wedding Days
What Do I Do? *(English/Spanish)*
What Do I Say?
Why Am I Different?

Text © 1989 by Norma Simon
Illustrations © 1989 by Helen Cogancherry
Published in 1989 by Albert Whitman & Company,
5747 West Howard, Niles, Illinois 60648
Published simultaneously in Canada by
General Publishing, Limited, Toronto
10 9 8 7 6 5 4 3 2 1

Library of Congress Cataloging-in-Publication Data
Simon, Norma.
I am not a crybaby / Norma Simon; pictures by Helen Cogancherry.
    p.   cm.
Summary: Children describe a variety of situations that make them
want to cry, emphasizing that crying is a normal reaction.
ISBN 0-8075-3447-1 (lib. bdg.)
1. Crying—Juvenile literature. 2. Crying in children—Juvenile
literature. [1. Crying.] I. Cogancherry, Helen, ill. II. Title.
BF575.C88S55 1989
155.4' 12—dc19   88-21698
                                                   CIP
                                                   AC

For my very special friends at Wellfleet Elementary School, with thanks for all you teach me.

Do you cry sometimes?
I am not a crybaby,
but when the kids choose up teams for baseball,
and I'm the last one picked, I want to cry.
I think no one likes me.
Well, how would you feel? What makes you cry?

I cried the time my skate stuck in a crack in the ice, and my leg broke. It really hurt! Dad carried me to our car and drove me to the hospital.

The doctor put a big cast on my leg.
Everyone signed the cast and decorated it.
It took a long time until I could skate again,
but pretty soon I felt better.

When we made plans to go to Disneyland,
and then I got chickenpox
and we couldn't go,
I was so disappointed, I cried.
My sister cried, too. We sniffled all afternoon.

I want to cry when people tease me
and call me names because I'm fat.
Making fun of people is a very mean thing to do.

When I was drying my mother's cake dish—the one her grandmother gave her—it dropped and broke into pieces. I felt awful! I cried for a long time. So did Mom. But she didn't yell at me or spank me.

She knew I felt sad enough.
I think I'll buy her a new cake dish
for Mother's Day.
I'll save up some of my allowance.

One time, my dad made me clean up my
room when I wanted to play with a friend.
He said my sister could play
even though *her* room was a mess!
I was so angry, I told him, "I hate you!"
Dad looked sad, and I started to cry.
I wished I could take the words back
because I really love my dad.

Big dogs barking
make me feel like crying.
They're scary.
My little sister isn't afraid at all.
She *likes* big barking dogs!

Bad dreams make me cry.
My mom comes to see what's wrong.
She tells me, "It's all right—
it was just a nightmare.
There's nothing to be afraid of."
She gives me a hug, and I go back to sleep.

Sometimes after school,
when I'm the only one home,
I'm so lonely I cry a little.
It helps when I play with our dog.
She's so happy to see me!
I think she gets lonely, too.

When my best friend
got a new best friend,
and I saw them together,
I couldn't hold back my tears.

I felt like crying the first day Mom left me
at a new school. I didn't know anybody.
Then my new teacher and all the children
told me their names. Mrs. Cooper put me next
to a nice boy named Tom.

When my mom came to pick me up,
I showed her my room, and I asked
if Tom could go home with us.
I was smiling.

Fighting makes me want to cry
even if I'm not in the fight!
I hate it when my brothers fight and swear,
and most of all, I hate it when my mom and dad fight.
After a while, I go into my bedroom and close the door
so I won't hear the awful words.

When you watch a friend move away, and you don't know when you'll see him again, don't you start to cry?

I want to see my friend Nick very much.
I hope he can visit soon. He's so far away!
We write letters, and for a treat, I call him
on the telephone.

My parents are divorced.
When I have to leave my dad
after we spend the weekend
together, I cry.
Dad looks sad, too.

I feel better when I get home and give him a call.

When my cat, Winston, died,
I cried and cried.
He was going across the road to hunt
when a car hit him.
My whole family was sad.
We made him a little gravestone.

I loved Winston because he never bit me or scratched me.
I would play games with him, and he let me dress him up.
He came when I called him. I still cry about my cat sometimes,
but I smile, too, when I remember the good times we had.

Do you ever see people cry because they're happy?
The day I got my hearing aid
and for the first time could hear
what everybody was saying,
my mom was so happy that tears came into her eyes.

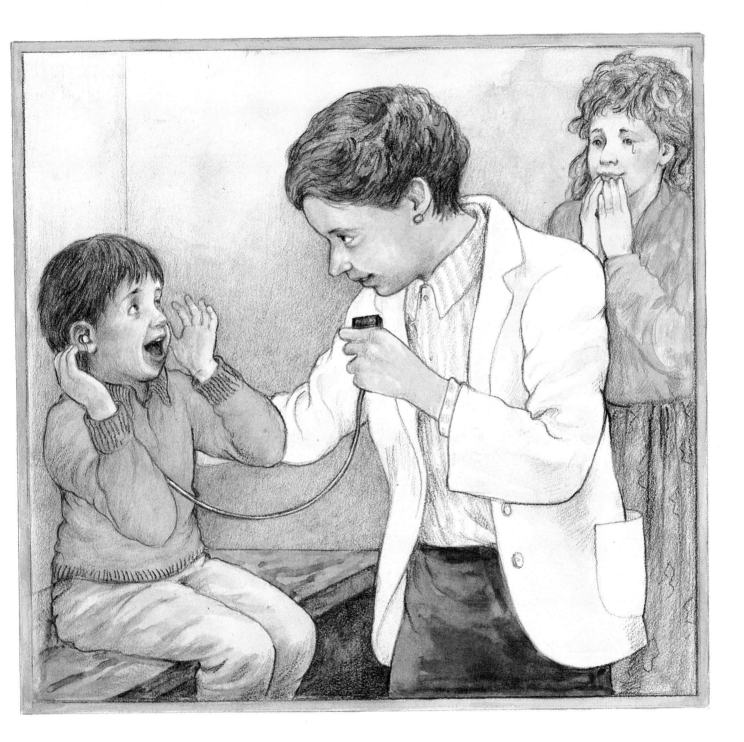

At weddings, people sometimes cry
and smile at the same time.
My grandma and grandpa smiled and cried
when Aunt Sue married Uncle Charlie.
They were so happy for Aunt Sue.
I didn't cry, but I was glad, too.

Sometimes when I watch the movie *Old Yeller*,
I cry during the part when Old Yeller dies.
It seems so real, as if Old Yeller is *my* dog.

I used to cry when I got a shot.
Now that I'm bigger, I just make a face.

Sometimes when I feel like crying,
I do. When I'm finished, I blow my nose and
wipe my face, and I feel better.

Sometimes when I feel like crying,
I don't because people are watching me,
and I want to act brave.
I'm glad I didn't cry when I fell off
my bike last week.

Everybody feels like crying sometimes.
Even my dad cries when sad things happen.
He says it's all right for big men and women to cry.
Teenagers cry, too, and old people.

Spanks and onions used to make me cry,"
my grandma told me.
"Now that I'm old, it's weddings, funerals,
and still, onions."

When you're crying
or when you feel like crying,
it's nice if someone hugs you.
A pat on the back is good, too.

I feel sorry for people
when they're sad and crying.
I hope they'll be better soon,
and I never say, "Crybaby!"